→ Police Kung Fu ←

THE PERSONAL COMBAT
HANDBOOK OF THE
TAIWAN NATIONAL POLICE

by Man Kam Lo

translated by
John Kang, Bradley Temple, and Nicholas Veitch

Tuttle Publishing
Boston • Rutland, Vermont • Tokyo

Disclaimer: Please note that the author and publisher of this book are NOT RESPONSIBLE in any manner whatsoever for any injury that may result from practicing the techniques and/or following the instructions given within. Since the physical activities described in this volume may be too strenuous in nature for some readers to engage in safely, *it is essential that a physician be consulted prior to training.*

First published by Tuttle Publishing, an imprint of Periplus Editions (HK) Ltd., with editorial offices at 153 Milk Street, Boston, Massachusetts 02109.

Library of Congress Cataloging-in-Publication Data

Lo, Man Kam, 1937-
   Police kung fu / by Man Kam Lo ; translated by John Kang.
     p. cm.
  ISBN 0-8048-3271-4 (pbk. : alk. paper)
   1. Self-defense for police. 2. Kung fu. I. Title.

HV8080.S34 L65 2001
613.6'6'0243632--dc21   2001042495

Distributed by

North America, Latin America, Europe
Tuttle Publishing
Distribution Center
Airport Industrial Park
364 Innovation Drive
North Clarendon, VT 05759-9436
Tel: (802) 773-8930
Toll free tel: (800) 526-2778
Fax: (802) 773-6993
Toll free fax: (800) 329-8885

Japan
Tuttle Publishing
RK Building, 2nd Floor
2-13-10 Shimo-Meguro, Meguro-Ku
Tokyo 153 0064
Tel: (03) 5437 0171
Fax: (03)5437 0755

Asia Pacific
Berkeley Books LTD
130 Joo Seng Road
#06-01/03
Olivine Building
Singapore 368357
Tel: (65) 280-1330
Fax: (65) 280-6290

05 04 03 02 01   9 8 7 6 5 4 3 2 1
Printed in the United States of America

Designed by Stephanie Doyle

KHURSHID
AHMED   TTT

→ **Contents** ←

TRANSLATORS' NOTE

As relatively junior students of Wing Chun Kung Fu Master Lo Man Kam (out of a family of 3,000 brothers and sisters that includes Taiwan movie star Brigitte Lin, Hong Kong pop-singer Samuel Tai, and the Sultan of Brunei), we were honored that Sifu Lo asked us to translate *Police Kung Fu*. As we enthusiastically dove into the job at hand, it soon became apparent that we would have to answer a lot of questions, and fill in a few gaps due to the context of the manual.

First published in 1993 under the title of "The Martial Arts of the Police," this book was intended for internal distribution within the Taiwan police academies. As such, the material, from the people named within to the very writing style, begins with the basic premise that the reader is a new police recruit who grew up within the Taiwan education system. It assumes that you understand certain linguistic usages, know who specific people are, and will be directly taught by a skilled instructor. However, these assumptions may not necessarily apply to you, the reader.

Therefore *Police Kung Fu* does not attempt to copy Sifu Lo's poetic style verbatim, but rather rearranges the rhythm of the text so that it flows logically in English. Chinese proverbs are noted as such, and famous people from Chinese history are further spelled out. Originally, the pictures had only brief descriptions, because a seasoned instructor would have demonstrated techniques firsthand; the explanations now contain much more detail to clear up possible ambiguities. Finally, since Sifu Lo believes that both people and their fighting styles should continually grow and evolve, he further opted to add new photographs and techniques to the English translation that would go into a future Chinese edition. So while this version is not an exact, word-for-word translation of "The Martial Arts of the Police," rest assured that it contains everything that Sifu Lo intended. We hope you enjoy his work.

John Kang, Bradley Temple, and Nicholas Veitch

FOREWORD

The duties of the police

Law enforcement officers must uphold public order, protect society, and promote the people's welfare. As defenders of the law, the police have the important responsibility to be teachers of right and wrong, and can be said to be the "guardian of the people." In pursuit of their noble cause, prospective police officers must have determination and be willing to sacrifice anything for the sake of justice. Most are young with high ideals, courage, and a true desire to move ever forward to improve themselves.

Self-improvement through serious endeavor

In this day and age, people are likely to embrace what is wrong and reject what is good. Many covet what they do not deserve, with no desire to attain goals through honest work. Some join gangs, use illegal drugs, and are thoroughly ensconced in laziness and decadence. They are involved in theft, robbery, and extortion, walking on the wrong side of the law without any fear of legal retribution. These people and their crimes are all threats to social order and stability. Police strive to fight crime, defend law-abiding citizens, and continually struggle against those who would break the law for their own selfish pleasures.

The primary tool of the police is martial skills, which they must develop through persistent practice. They must continually seek to improve their abilities, constantly cultivating the essential qualities of prudence, ferocity, courage, and correct judgment. Even after years of learning, one can achieve only a superficial level.

Continuous practice to hone skills to perfection; complacency leads to deterioration of skill.

Fighting techniques must be continuously practiced and refined. The police officer must develop martial skills through constant combat practice and body conditioning. Whether training involves contact sparring or choreographed drills, the ultimate goal is to develop skills capable of overwhelming the most ferocious opponent. For when the day comes that he must actually use these skills in a real situation, the police officer must have a simple but effective repertoire of techniques that he can call upon naturally and instinctively. In combat, one must grasp four principles: fighting time, fighting position, fighting distance, and correct use of surroundings. The goal of combat training is to hone these tools, so that when facing a criminal, the officer will know the best time and place to attack, without having to panic and rush. When the officer attacks, he must act with power, confidence, and speed so as to intimidate the criminal into submission. Only in readiness can his fighting spirit be expressed.

Rectifying wrongs over time, to elevate the position of the police

The analogous ideas of "using laws to govern society" and "using technique to control an opponent" are different approaches to achieving the same goals. However, while "laws" are set through the cooperation of a representative body, martial skills are "passed down" from teacher to student, and further refined through practice. Laymen without such skill cannot contribute to the learning process, and the concept of "passing down" from master to student must be honored with the deepest sincerity.

The police officer must train continuously, endeavoring to develop abilities to achieve a state of perfection. Through the practice of superior martial techniques, he may rectify the wrongs of this world, and help to elevate the police in the public eye.

Continuous practice, strength through unity

Master Lo Man Kam is a true practitioner of Wing Chun, directly inheriting the tradition from Grandmaster Yip Man. He is one of the most advanced in martial arts circles, having already attained a profound level of achievement. Since receiving the honor of teaching the Peace Preservation Corps, Master Lo has shared everything with his students, without reservation. He is truly a model coach. His book *Police Kung Fu* embodies the essence of martial techniques.

This said, I have the honor of expressing my deepest appreciation and gratitude toward Master Lo for the publication of this book. I would like to stress the importance of continuous practice in an attempt to reach perfection, and hope that the reader will always remind himself of this fact. If all law enforcement officers can grasp the essentials of this book, the dregs of our society will tremble at our name. Righteousness must triumph over evil.

Lu Yu-sheng
Ministry of Interior, Police Chief
July 30, 1993

PROLOGUE

Prospective police officers must first complete a set course of study before gaining a mandate to serve. Besides having extensive knowledge of the law, police officers must also understand unarmed and armed martial skills, so that when facing any situation in the pursuit of their work, they can respond effectively and efficiently.

The martial aspects of police curricula include Judo, Tae Kwon Do, and other assorted techniques such as grappling, use of the police club, and skills for arresting a suspect. This curriculum undergoes revisions from time to time, to suit the needs of the police force in their ultimate goal of maintaining public order.

The author of this book, Master Lo Man Kam, has a profound understanding of martial arts, having studied Choy Li Fut kung fu under Master Chan Lu in Futshan, Canton, and later Wing Chun kung fu with his maternal uncle, the Grandmaster Yip Man. He is the third elder kung fu brother of martial arts legend Bruce Lee, and has continuously studied the fighting arts to enhance his already deep understanding.

Master Lo was born in Hong Kong, and later moved to Taiwan, where he graduated from Shihpai Military Academy and served in the Ministry of Defense as a martial arts instructor. He has also worked in the intelligence department of the Ministry of Defense, taught the Dominican

Republic's ambassador to the Republic of China, is an instructor of martial arts at the Chinese Culture University, and further trained members of the Special Investigation Department, Ministry of Justice. He currently holds the position of instructor to both the police SWAT teams and the bodyguards to the president, as well as being a member of the Chinese Kuo-Shu Federation Development Committee.

Besides this book, Master Lo has also published textbooks on basic Wing Chun kung fu and articles on Wing Chun techniques and self-defense. Outside of martial arts circles, he has also published articles in the monthly *Mainland China Studies* on mainland industries.

Police Kung Fu can give the reader new insights on martial arts, taking into consideration the concept of using natural human motions and enhancing martial theory with physics. His theories indeed correspond to strategies of war and military principles. The chapters of this book include "How to Train for Hand-to-Hand Combat," "Techniques Against a Knife," "Techniques Against a Gun," "Use of the Police Club," and "Unarmed Combat"; these form the basis of the police curriculum.

Liu Shou-de
Peace Preservation Corps
Taipei, Summer 1993

INTRODUCTION
TO THE AUTHOR

Instructor: Lo Man Kam
Birth: Hong Kong, May 25, 1937
Military Training: Shihpai Military Academy, 1st Division,
                           13th Class
Military Experience: Anti-Communism Committee, Overseas Bureau
                       Army 84th Battalion (Sergeant Major)
                       Ministry of Defense, Intelligence Division
Martial Arts: Wing Chun kung fu, from Grandmaster
                           Yip Man
Other notes: Professor, Chinese Culture University, Taipei
                       Instructor to the R.O.C. Peace Preservation Corps
                       Police SWAT Team Instructor (unarmed combat
                           coach), Ministry of Justice Special
                           Investigation Bureau
                       Member, R.O.C. Kuo-Shu Federation
                           Development Division
                       Unarmed Combat Coach, R.O.C. Police
                           College
                       Wing Chun Instructor, Embassy of the
                           Dominican Republic, R.O.C.

→ **1** ←

HOW TO TRAIN FOR
HAND-TO-HAND COMBAT

Effective martial techniques rely upon spontaneous, instinctive reflexes, with movement natural to human physiology serving as a foundation. Such fighting skills do not resemble athletics and are even less akin to choreographed movement set to rhythm or music, in that fluidity takes precedence over rote technique. When embarking on a study of police martial arts, the officer must begin by taking a broader perspective, remembering that there are multiple ways to effectively counter any given movement. In essence, he must learn to blend his own natural reflexes with acquired martial techniques.

Understanding Police Martial Techniques

The fighting system employed by the Taiwan police takes Wing Chun kung fu and natural physiological function as its basis. Integrating physics, geometry, and other scientific principles to unite the body with motion, it stresses fluidity to enable unlimited fighting force in combat. The techniques do not employ the methodology of traditional Chinese kung fu, which trains individual moves and counters, nor do they imitate the animal movements of some Mainland Chinese martial styles. Unlike the choreographed movements in martial arts films, they place little emphasis on physical strength and beauty. All such training turns the student into an automaton, lacking the flexibility to deal with an ever-changing combat situation.

Police martial arts stress the principle of "bringing dead technique to life." Copied as set rigid routines, individual techniques remain "dead," and therefore incapable of adapting to sudden changes. Human beings are alive, and they rarely adhere to a script; fluidity allows for multiple options and the ability to accommodate fluctuations in a combat situation. It overcomes the limitations imposed by inflexible mechanical movement and eliminates the need to memorize Chinese martial movements with over-embellished titles such as, "eagle opens its wings," "tiger comes down mountain," "dragonfly touches water," and so on.

Rather, the police fighting style stresses understanding of the martial principles of fighting distance, fighting position, and fighting time. Understanding and mastery of distance means knowing what techniques work at what range and how to control the space between exponent and adversary. Unlike distance, which focuses on range, position takes into account fighting stance, angle of attack, and awareness of the environment and terrain. Timing includes rhythm, flow of attack, and taking initiative. The practitioner can take a proactive approach, thereby forcing his opponent into passive reactions.

These principles enhance technique. Synthesizing the advantages of the officer's own physique, the techniques permit ease of response by employing natural human movement. Further, police martial arts do not rely upon passive, reactive attacks. Instead they adopt the approach of the famous general Sun Tzu, who wrote in *The Art of War,* "the most effective defense is offense." To rely on offense, police officers must also have the appropriate frame of mind and adhere to such principles as, "when the enemy is still, use the opportunity to move," and "when the enemy moves, react with unlimited fighting power."

To reiterate, training for police martial techniques does not place value on appearance, nor rely upon repetition of unchanging mechanical movement, or the theatrical, impractical forms of modern Mainland Chinese Wu Shu.

Understanding and Practice

Keeping in mind the importance of martial power, the student should continually practice technique applications. In addition to combining individual techniques, the practitioner must further develop fluidity in order to integrate kung fu with his physiology and thought processes. Merely perusing books or diagrams to learn kung fu may be a superficially pleasing approach, but it is, in fact, a mistake. One simple analogy is a field commander trying to rely upon a book of tactics to make up for lack of practical experience. Such a commander will most likely fail on the battlefield. Let us say you are a track and field athlete and yet you do not regularly practice at the track. How will you achieve a breakthrough in your performance? Even worse is the person who just reads about track and field. How can such a person possibly improve his speed by simply reading?

Only constant practical training enables the exponent to confront an enemy and bring into play unlimited fighting power. The Chinese saying: "the more sweat in times of peace, the less blood in times of war" sums up this idea. Only through persistent practice of techniques can a police officer achieve a high proficiency in maintaining fighting position, distance, attack timing, and other major factors. In battle he can then immediately discern advantageous terrain, objects, and the distance between himself and the enemy, and, through application of appropriate movements, he can have both tactical advantage and effective martial power.

Conclusion

First waiting to see how an enemy moves, then spending added time determining which technique or form to counter with, is passive and invariably results in failure. Even if the officer does react with an effective move, he is still just reacting and is thus one step behind the opponent. This becomes especially problematic when considering all the different styles of Chinese kung fu. No student knows every movement from every style. In fact, fluidity of movement is always superior to fixed techniques that match a "dead" move with each of the opponent's "dead" moves. Therein lies the problem created by relying upon the descriptions and pictures in books and learning a "dead" version of kung fu: one falls victim to the problem of first having to consider what to do, then reacting with counter moves—this is just much too slow. Reliance upon pictures alone is even worse, as, without practical experience, a student unavoidably develops an inaccurate conception of real fighting. Teaching movements orchestrated to commands is just choreography. Such movement cannot be applied during a real encounter.

It cannot be overstated that only practical training in controlled but realistic fighting situations provides the student with a proper framework for learning. With physical contact, he can apply and improve upon what has already been learned. Then, in a real conflict, he has immediate, effective, flexible responses that have unlimited applications.

As a police officer, I have been in situations during my service when I have suddenly been outnumbered and attacked by criminals or ruffians. In the knowledge that disadvantageous situations will inevitably arise from time to time, I have been diligent in my training and always trained with live, mock opponents. As a result, I have consistently reacted both immediately and effectively in sudden dangerous situations. I have applied flexible, automatic responses to defeat my opponents and not relied upon imitating dead illustrations found in books. This is the road to success in combat.

→ **II** ←

TECHNIQUES
AGAINST A KNIFE

The most important aspect of fighting against a knife-wielding opponent is using the correct techniques in the quickest and most efficient way to counter and control the adversary, while at the same time minimizing the risk of injury to oneself. When suddenly placed in such a situation, the police officer must make the most of his fighting distance and fighting position. Correct application of these concepts, combined with proper timing, will allow you to protect yourself from harm. In addition to gaining a superior fighting position when facing a criminal armed with a bladed weapon, regardless of its shape or size, you must remain calm and relaxed. As an old Chinese classic says, "A settled mind leads to calm, calm leads to relaxation, relaxation leads to clear thought, clear thought leads to achievement of goals." It is only when you are calm and relaxed that you can think and react effectively, preventing rash decisions that may have fatal consequences. Therefore, you must prepare yourself mentally, vanquishing your fear when facing a knife, or else you will be unable overcome your foe.

The best way to conquer this fear is through preparation in everyday training, specifically with the use of a real weapon in practice sessions. Start by having your training partner wave a bladed weapon in front of you at a distance, gradually increasing the proximity and speed of the motion. Keep your eyes open no matter how close the weapon comes. As you become more comfortable, begin using real knives in the drills you are most familiar with, at a very slow pace, and progressively build up speed. Remember that in such drills, cooperation and partnership are of the utmost importance, and any bravado or macho attitudes can lead to injury. After training in such a manner, you should have gained the confidence to face a knife-wielding suspect in the line of duty. In all actions, you must grasp the idea: "Should the enemy attack, I will react with unlimited martial power."

Criminal records reveal that bladed weapons typically used in crimes include household knives, combat knives, switchblades, machetes, etc. They can be further classified according to length and function; for example, swords and machetes are all large-sized slashing knives, while switchblades and buck knives are concealable short-range weapons. As the shapes and sizes of knives are different, so are their usages in inflicting harm. A short, sharp knife's most probable angle of attack is a frontal thrust or an overhand stab. For long, single-edged knives, overhead chops and quick, angular slashes are common. Therefore, when an officer sees what type of blade his opponent is using, he can predict the manner in which it will be used.

It is imperative that you do not rush, and never try to struggle for the weapon. Do not try to disarm the suspect if you are not close enough: you could face avoidable bodily harm. Our purpose is to arrest the suspect while avoiding unnecessary injury. Keep the best fighting position, and coordinate the use of hands and feet. No matter which way you fight, only try to control his weapon hand and constrain his movement, using the skills that you have developed. Do not plan your techniques, because your enemy will not follow a script. Instead, use the instincts that you have refined in training. You should prepare for any kind of situation during class.

In addition, you must persistently hone your skills of controlling, penetrating, pressing, kicking, and grappling, and apply them according to the given situation. In this way, your techniques will become "live," and will enable you to exploit limitless options, thereby increasing your fighting prowess. Your techniques must not be passive or set, for that is "dead" kung fu, and may lead to your own injury. When you face an opponent, you should rely only on those techniques that you are familiar with from practice, and use them in combination according to the ever-changing situation.

While your ultimate goal is arresting a suspect, you must take your own personal safety into consideration.

Remember that you must not depend purely upon strength or speed to control your opponent, because if he is stronger or faster, he will be able to overpower you. Accordingly, you must not struggle for control of the knife, for that is a passive position. Although that may work in a movie or exhibition, reality may prove to be different. Therefore, you must face the opponent using continuous and ever-changing attacks, so as not to give him an opportunity to initiate his own attack. The best methods of attack are opposite shoulder-to-shoulder and cross shoulder-to-shoulder. Either way should use parallel structure to bleed off attacks instead of direct blocking. (See photos below.) Once again, I want to emphasize that the most efficient approach is continuous, changing attacks.

→ SERIES 1 ←

Holding a knife in this manner, the suspect will most likely strike with a straight downward stab or an angled downward stab. The direction will depend on your body positioning. In this case, you are standing a little to the inside in a shoulder-to-shoulder position, and the likely line of attack will be angled. Be prepared for him to switch his hand position, possibly to his left for a left-to-right slash.

This particular technique is an attack on the opponent's shoulder joint.

1–1   Against an overhead stab. . .

1–2   As the attacker thrusts with an overhead stab, face him shoulder-to-shoulder and use your left hand to intercept at the inside of his hand.

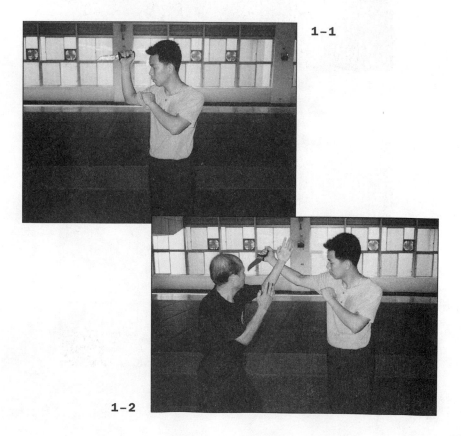

1–1

1–2

1-3 Your right hand cuts upwards so that the blade of your forearm hits right behind the opponent's elbow joint.

1-4 Grasp the wrist with both hands and pull down.

1-3

1-4

✦ SERIES 2 ✦

Like the first series, this one assumes that you stop your opponent's weapon further away from your body, thereby allowing space for your other hand to slide forward comfortably. This attack begins with an attack on the shoulder joint before shifting to a wrist lock, and finally to an elbow/wrist lock combination.

2–1   Facing the knifeman shoulder-to-shoulder, intercept with your left hand to the inside of the knife hand.

2–2   Thrust your right hand directly toward the right side of the opponent's neck, placing your palm on the back of his neck.

2–1

2–2

2-3 Pivot out on your left leg. While controlling the knife hand, pull him down into a right knee strike to the body.

2-4 Your right hand moves back to grasp and control the attacker's hand.

2-3

2-4

2-5

2-6

2-5 Use both hands to twist his wrist clockwise and into his body.

2-6 Apply pressure to the elbow joint with a right arm bar, to push his body over.

⇥ SERIES 3 ⇤

When holding a knife in this fashion, the attacker has limited his options. The most likely attack will be a straight stab. The counter detailed herein uses the Wing Chun tan sao (palm up) to redirect the line of attack, while the turn in the hips gives more power to the attack to the neck. The striking conveniently leads to a shoulder-joint attack. See Series 7 for a similar technique.

3–1 Against a forward thrust with the knife. . .

3–2 From cross-shoulder facing position, block the attack with an inside tan sao deflection.

3–1

3–2

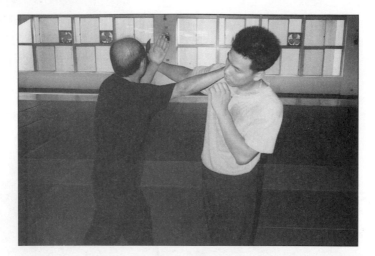

3–3

3–4

3–3 Turning your hips, thrust forward with a right hand-slash to the neck.

3–4 Your right hand slides down the opponent's arm to the elbow, to lock the joint, while your other hand simultaneously rises and pushes his hand back into him.

3–5 Step to the attacker's right side while continuing to apply pressure to the opponent's knife hand and pulling the elbow upwards.

3–6 Shift your position to the opponent's rear and deliver a kick to the back of the knee.

3–5

3–6

✦ SERIES 4 ✦

Unlike Series 1, this one starts off with you facing your opponent cross-shoulder. If you move to his outside gate as the encounter begins, you are again limiting his possible attacks. This particular example shows a high to low, inside to out stab, though be careful that he doesn't shift to a lower horizontal stab. As you complete your deflection, you begin a shoulder joint attack; he will most likely try to resist, giving you a chance to borrow his force and pull him into an elbow lock. You end by using a knee to apply pressure to the shoulder joint, thereby freeing your hand.

4–1 Against the forward knife thrust, shift to a cross-shoulder position and intercept to the outer gate.

4–1

4–2 Cover the elbow with your left hand while pushing your right hand forward to wrap around the arm and press his wrist into the shoulder joint.

4–3 As he naturally fights against the power of your position, redirect his force by pulling his arm with a controlled downward lateral motion and pushing the elbow so that it turns over. Remember to step off to his right side.

4–2

4–3

4–4   As your body reaches his right side, press down on his elbow joint to achieve control.

4–5   Your left hand returns to his hand while you press your knee down into his elbow joint.

4–6   Disarm the enemy with a sweeping motion of your left hand.

4–4

4–5

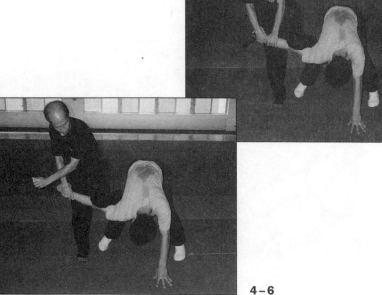

4–6

→ SERIES 5 ←

While Series 3 uses a block to the inside gate, this technique makes use of Wing Chun's gong sao (lower sweeping right block combined with upper sweeping left block) to redirect the line of attack. With both of your hands in contact with your opponent, they can be easily used for joint-locking purposes, this time for twisting the wrist joint. Note that as you pull, your opponent will resist, most likely by pulling back, allowing you to use his energy to throw him with the joint lock.

5-1 Facing a forward thrust from a cross-shoulder position. . .

5-2 Execute a low-lying gong sao while stepping to the side with your left foot and pivoting your body out of his knife's line.

5-1

5-2

5-3   Your left hand slides down the attacker's arm, so that both of your hands control the knife hand. The pull should disrupt his balance.

5-4   Pull the enemy's hand up and start to twist over to your left.

5-3

5-4

5–5

5–5 Continue twisting outward while supporting your structure with a right step forward...

5–6 thereby throwing the opponent down.

5–6

☞ SERIES 6 ☜

In Series 5, if you step forward with your left foot instead of to the side, you can use a kuan sao (right palm-up tan sao combined with left wing arm bong sao). With both of your hands in contact with his arm, and room to step into his stance with your left foot, you may conveniently use leverage in this elbow-joint attack.

6-1   Starting from cross-shoulder position, the opponent steps forward with a straight knife thrust. Stepping to the side and into a shoulder-to-shoulder position, deflect the oncoming attack with a kuan sao (right outside parry combined with left arm level, roughly parallel to the ground).

6-1

6–2   As your left arm slides in to help your right hand control his knife hand, turn your body into the opponent and pull his arm down, using your shoulder as a fulcrum against the spot behind his elbow.

6–3   Starting with your right leg, step back behind the opponent; slide your left hand out, and wrap your elbow into the pressure point behind his elbow. Finish by pushing him down.

6–2

6–3

⇥ SERIES 7 ⇤

Slashing weapons are versatile and have many different angles of attack. However, the positioning of your body relative to your opponent's will once again help limit his attacks. Here, the suspect is slashing downward, either at an angle or vertically. This technique resembles Series 3, albeit used against a slash. The joint lock is taken one step further, to the point where you stretch his triceps so he turns around.

7-1   Against an overhead slash with a watermelon knife (or machete)...

7-2   Stepping forward with your left foot into a shoulder-to-shoulder position, block to the inside of his arm with your left hand, while your right hand contacts his upper arm.

7-1

7-2

7 – 3 Chop across the attacker's arm toward his neck, using your right arm.

7 – 4 Slide your hand back over the enemy's arm to the elbow joint, while pushing your left hand forward and back into the opponent.

7 – 5 (close-up)

7 – 3

7 – 4

7 – 5

7-6 Continue pushing with the same motion, thereby forcing the opponent to turn around so that his back is to you.

7-7 Kick the back of his knee with your right leg.

7-8 Continue the motion in order to obtain full control.

7-6

7-7

7-8

→ SERIES 8 ←

As in Series 7, your position will limit your opponent's attack options. This particular technique works against vertical or angled downward slashes, and even better against outside-to-inside sweeping attacks. Here, you are using the energy generated by your turn to both redirect the opponent's attack and add force to your attack. The closing also shows that we can use our legs to provide leverage.

8-1 Against an overhead slash. . .

8-2 Step forward so that you are shoulder-to-shoulder, deflecting the attacker's knife arm on the inside with your left hand, while beginning a round sweeping attack with your other hand.

8-1

8-2

8-3   Your body rotates counterclockwise while stepping with the right foot behind the opponent's right lead leg.

8-4   Your right arm connects to the opponent's throat...

8-3

8-4

8–5   Clipping the opponent over your own leg (reverse angle).

8–6   Making sure his arm is straight, use your left leg as a fulcrum for leverage against the knife arm.

8–5

8–6

8–7 Strike towards his groin with your right hand.

8–8 Bring your right hand back to prepare...

8–9 For a chop to the enemy's wrist to disarm him.

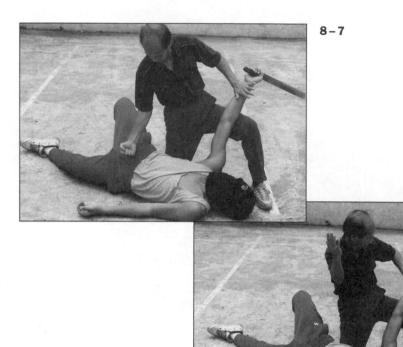

8–7

8–8

8–9

✦ SERIES 9 ✦

This technique resembles Series 1, though used against a slash.

9–1   Stand shoulder-to-shoulder, against an overhead outside-to-inside slash.

9–2   Step forward with your left foot, while blocking to the inside of his hand with your left hand.

9–1

9–2

9-3 Using your right forearm bone, thrust up into the pressure point behind his elbow.

9-4 Threading through with your right hand, take control of his forearm with a pull down.

9-5 (close-up)

9-3

9-4

9-5

⋆ SERIES 10 ⋆

This technique counters either a vertical or angled downward attack, and depends on positioning your body outside of the cutting line. The interception leads directly into a shoulder-joint attack, supported by a knee so as to free a hand for disarming.

10-1 Facing off in a shoulder-to-shoulder stance. . .

10-2 As the attacker comes in and slashes down, step to the outside of his lead leg with your right foot, and prepare to block to the outer side of his knife hand.

10-1

10-2

10-3   Complete the block and make contact.

10-4   Pivot around on your left lead leg to move behind the opponent, pulling forward on his arm with your right hand and pressing your left forearm into his shoulder joint; lean forward to add pressure and tighten the angle.

10-3

10-4

10-5

10-5   Continue downward pressure to force your opponent down.

10-6   Insert your knee into his shoulder joint while your left arm slides up his arm to control and disarm.

10-6

⇥ **SERIES 11** ⇤

This counter is similar to Series 6, but here it is used against a downward slash. You may finish with a technique similar to 6–3 as well.

11–1   From a shoulder-to-shoulder position against an overhead hack. . .

11–2   Use your right hand to block to the outside of the opponent's arm.

11–1

11–2

11-3 Taking control of his arm with both of your hands, turn on your right foot and step into the opponent's body with your left leg.

11-4 Control his knife hand with both hands while pulling down, using your shoulder as a fulcrum.

11-3

11-4

→ SERIES 12 ←

A slashing weapon can be used to cut from inside to out, at varying angles. If you can close the distance soon enough, you can trap your opponent's elbow to jam the attack before it even gets started. Otherwise, if you move to the outside of his lead leg, you will catch the attack later in its trajectory, which can allow you to use this technique. Here, you are once again using, and then redirecting, his force.

12-1   Facing cross-shoulder, your opponent prepares to attack with a long blade.

12-2   He slashes from middle to high, inside to outside.

12-3   Block the opponent's slash with an outer block, while stepping out with your left foot.

12-4   Following the opponent's force, press his elbow in with your left hand while rotating your own right arm into an arm bar, to lock his arm.

12-3

12-4

12-5 Wrench the opponent's elbow up while pulling his hand downward to force the blade into the opponent's neck.

12-6 Deliver a right kick to the back of his knee.

12-5

12-6

→ III ←

TECHNIQUES
AGAINST A GUN

In the hands of criminals, firearms can cause all kinds of headaches for society. Their appearance can rapidly transform a normal situation into panic, putting fear in people's hearts and escalating tensions. The ever-increasing numbers of guns on the street have led to a lack of faith in social order and made criminals even more confident. Use of firearms in many felonies—Mafia struggles over territory, illegal drug transactions, revenge, murder, hijacking, and even government suppression—has become rather prevalent. Whether in a simple drug bust or in negotiations with armed suspects who are cornered and have taken hostages, police will inevitably come into contact with guns in their line of work. Therefore, martial techniques against guns are an essential part of the law enforcement officer's curriculum.

No matter how simple or complicated the situation, the police officer must know these skills and the position and distance at which they work. Techniques against guns work only at close range, and the officer must execute them from a favorable position with appropriate speed. It must be remembered that the man with the gun has the advantage in terms of reaction time, as it takes him less time to move his finger when pulling a trigger than it does for his opponent to move his entire body. Therefore, do not count purely upon speed when trying to overcome a gun-wielding opponent. Rather, try to put yourself in a position of minimal danger, where the gunman's line of site is obstructed, and move when the enemy is least able to react. Surprise is the most ideal method for disarming a suspect armed with a firearm.

In addition, when moving to disarm a gun-wielding opponent at close range, it does not matter what part of your body the gun is pointed at, or whether or not the opponent is directly facing you. You must always remember that when you initiate your attack, your own body must turn at an angle out of line with the gun. In this way, you can minimize bodily injury should the opponent fire. It cannot be overemphasized that the goal is to safely disarm the suspect, and not to directly attack him or simply knock him down without considering the position of his gun. Further, care must be taken so that no bystanders are in the weapon's line of fire in the event that it is discharged. Lastly, when you have gained control of the gun, you must take one or two steps backward, with the weapon pointed at your opponent. This way, you can maintain safe distance between the gun and the enemy, and prevent him from trying to take the gun back.

If you cannot put yourself at an effective distance or advantageous position from which you can gain control of the gun, you must think of a means to lull the suspect into the belief that you will not make a move. In this way, you give yourself opportunities by using psychological tactics either to force the suspect into surrender, distract his attention, or alter his line of sight. Feigning submission or reminding the suspect of his actions' consequences are opposite extremes, yet both may effect the desired response. Therefore, the use of martial techniques in tandem with psychological warfare may be a way of overcoming an otherwise disadvantageous situation.

When faced with a gun pointing at you, you must maintain the calm and clarity developed through constant practice, expediently trying to reach an advantageous fighting distance. Use of psychological warfare is of the utmost importance, as is attempting to distract your enemy's attention. Even so, the best way is not to have to rely on fighting techniques at all, but to find other means of bringing about the suspect's surrender.

⤳ **SERIES 1** ⤶

With a gun pointed at your back, you are at a serious disadvantage. However, given the proximity, you are already in range to execute your attack. You must use psychological means to give you the element of surprise when you move to attack, and remember that turning your body at an angle will move you out of the gunman's line of fire, or at least minimize the area that will be hit.

1-1   The gunman is pressing his weapon into your lower back.

1-2   Turn left 180 degrees out of his line of fire, sliding your left arm to the outside of his elbow and trapping his hand against your upper arm. Simultaneously strike toward his face.

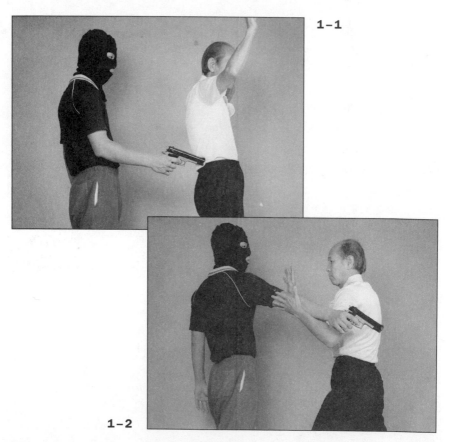

1-1

1-2

1-3 Finished movement.

1-4 As you start twisting your waist to the left, maintain a hold on the gunman's elbow with your left hand, while your right hand slides down his arm...

1-5 Catching the back of the gun.

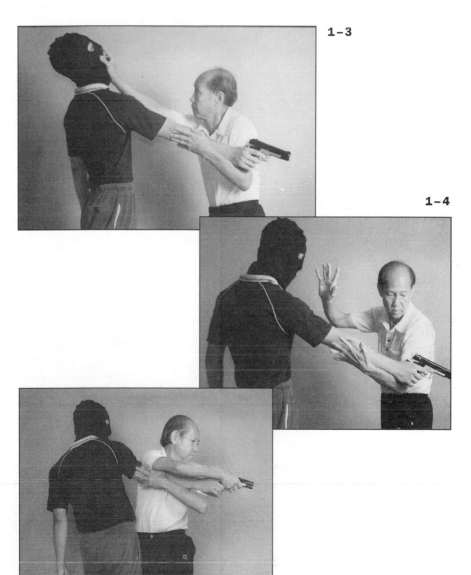

1-3

1-4

1-5

1-6

1-7

1-6 As you finish your twist, step through with your left foot and continue the motion to disarm him.

1-7 Pivot out on your left foot and take a couple of steps backwards while pointing the gun at him.

→ SERIES 2 ←

As in Knife Series 5, your Wing Chun gang sao puts your hands in position to control the weapon. In this series, you are turning to the outside of the arm, instead of the inside as in Series 1.

2-1   The opponent presses the gun into your upper back.

2-2   Pivot to the right while executing a high and low gang sao (low right sweeping block combined with left upper cross block) to move out of the gun's line of fire.

2-1

2-2

2-3   Bring your right hand and left hand back to the opponent's gun hand.

2-4   Twist his wrist counterclockwise and apply forward pressure into his body, making sure that the gun's barrel never crosses your body.

2-3

2-4

2-5

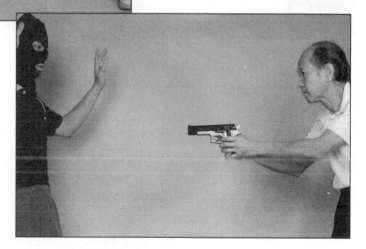

2-6

2-5 Maintain firm control of his gun hand with your left hand while stepping in with your right foot and using your right hand to slide the gun out.

2-6 Take a couple of steps backward while turning the gun on the suspect.

⇥ **SERIES 3** ⇤

Despite the gunman's two-handed grip, the principles remain the same. This particular technique resembles Series 2; however, the gang sao is eliminated. Remember to control the trigger hand with the leverage of your lock.

3–1 Holding the gun with two hands, the gunman points the weapon into your back.

3–2 Pivot outside to the right while sliding your hands down his arm to control his hands.

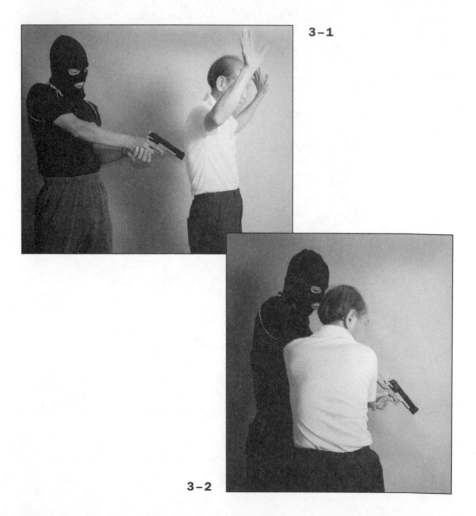

3–1

3–2

3–3

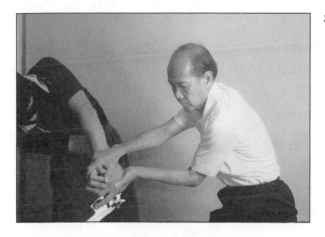

3–3 Stepping back with your left foot, twist his wrist counterclockwise, maintaining attention on the hand holding the gun.

3–4 Disarm the gunman, using a sweeping right-hand motion across the top of his hands. Remember to finish by taking a few steps back.

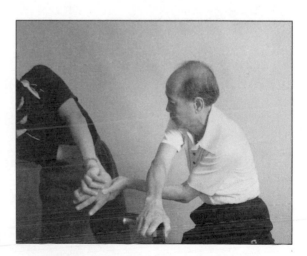

3–4

⁜ SERIES 4 ⁜

Unlike the previous situations, this one starts off with you standing face to face with the opponent, just outside of your technique's effective range. You must make the gunman think that he is in full control before moving into range for attack. The joint lock remains the same as in Series 3.

4-1   With a two-handed grip, the gunman is pointing his firearm directly at you.

4-2   Step in while turning your body to the left, out of the gun's line of fire, moving to control his hands.

4-1

4-2

4 – 3 Twist his wrist counterclockwise, while applying pressure into his body so the gun now points at him.

4 – 4 Slide your hand forward to disarm your opponent.

4 – 5 Take a few steps back, reversing the situation.

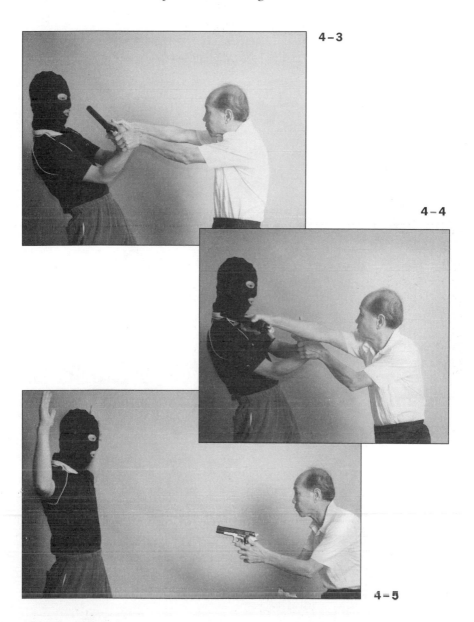

4 – 3

4 – 4

4 – 5

⇥ SERIES 5 ⇤

This technique begins like Series 4, but this time you continue twisting his locked wrist to the outside.

5–1 The gunman is pointing his weapon directly at you.

5–2 Turn your body out to the left, out of the line of fire, while going for control of his hand.

5–1

5–2

5-3 Twist his wrist outward, counterclockwise; your force may be able to force him to the ground.

5-4 Push your hand forward and take his gun away.

5-5 Take a few steps back and point the gun at him.

5-3

5-4

5-5

↝ **SERIES 6** ↜

While this technique begins like Gun Series 4 and 5, it uses the same principles as Knife Series 5 to bring the opponent to the ground. You are once again using his resistance to redirect your opponent's energy.

6–1 The gunman is pointing the gun directly at you, holding the weapon with one hand.

6–2 Turn your body outside to the left, while going for control of his gun with both hands.

6–1

6–2

6 – 3 Swiftly pull up on the opponent's wrist, causing him to lose his balance.

6 – 4 Twist his wrist outward, counterclockwise.

6 – 5 Continue your twist, causing him to lose his balance.

6 – 3

6 – 4

6 – 5

6-6 While the opponent is on the ground, continue controlling his hand.

6-7 Push him down with your right foot while sweeping your hand back to your body and disarming him in the process.

6-8 Step back and point the gun at him.

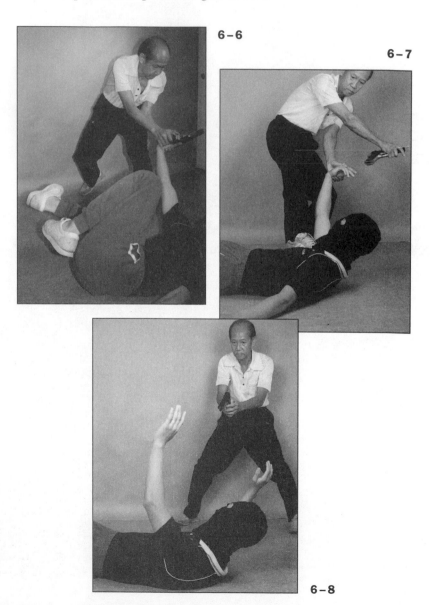

6-6

6-7

6-8

⤜ **SERIES 7** ⤛

In some cases, the gunman may demand that you get on the floor. Consciously choose which knee you will go down on, for it will have a bearing on which techniques you can use to counter. Resembling knife techniques 6 and 11, this series is facilitated by your standing motion.

7-1 With a one hand grip, the suspect points his gun into your upper back.

7-2 Following his orders, go to a kneeling position.

7-1

7-2

7–3 Kneeling on the left leg...

7–4 Stand up while pivoting to the right on your right leg, simultaneously pushing his arm away from your body with your right arm.

7–5 Step into the center of his body while sliding your left hand under his gun arm.

7–3

7–4

7–5

7-6   Turn into his body, take control of his hand with both of your hands, and press down, using your own shoulder as the fulcrum of a lever.

7-7   Disarm him, using your left hand.

7-8   Pivot out, taking a few steps back, and point the gun at him.

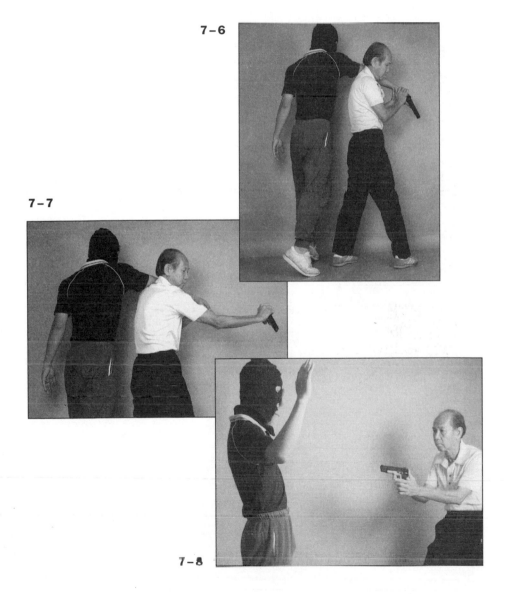

7-6

7-7

7-8

→ SERIES 8 ←
(reverse angle, from 7–5)

Alternately, if the opponent is much taller, you may bring your entire body under his arm.

8–1   Turn your body under his arm while controlling his gun with both of your hands.

8–2   Thrust your hips backward, thereby stretching his arm and causing him to lose his grip on the gun.

8–3   Twist your body out, take a few steps backward, and point the weapon at him.

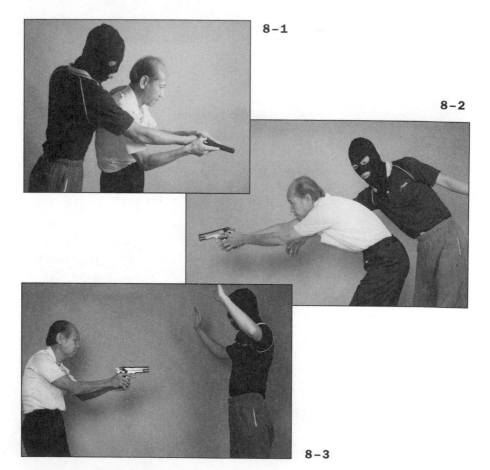

8–1

8–2

8–3

→ SERIES 9 ←
(on the stairs)

In some cases, you will be at a further disadvantage due to uneven ground or tight space. Still, the principles remain the same, and this technique is executed similarly to Gun Series 6 and Knife Series 5 in that you are borrowing your opponent's energy—he will instinctively pull back against the pull so that he does not fall down the steps.

9-1   The opponent is standing above you to the right, with his gun pointed into your ribs.

9-2   Twist your body to the right, while deflecting his gun with a right sweeping low gong sao, so you are no longer in his line of fire.

9-1

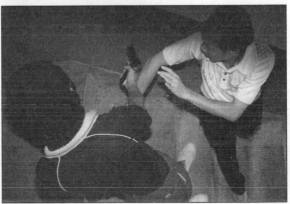

9-2

9–3

9–3   Take control of his hand with both of yours.

9–4   Turn his wrist counterclockwise, taking care not to allow the line of fire to pass over your body.

9–4

9-5

9-5 Disarm him with a sweeping motion of your right hand.

9-6 Take a few steps down, and point the gun at him.

9-6

⇗ SERIES 10 ⇖

Again in a tight space, this technique begins like Series 7, and ends like Series 9.

10-1   On the stairs, the opponent is standing above you and pointing the gun at the base of your skull.

10-2   Turn your body to the right, deflecting his weapon with your raised arms.

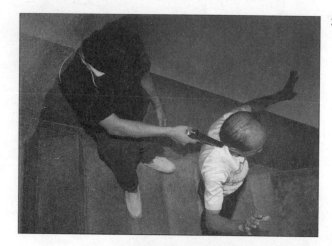

10-1

10-2

10-3 Take control of his gun hand, right hand on top, left hand on bottom.

10-4 Step to the right while pulling him forward, causing him to lose his balance.

10-5 Pull him down.

10-3

10-4

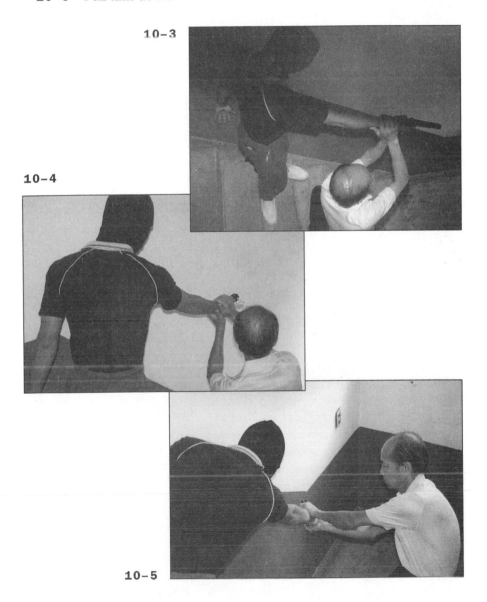

10-5

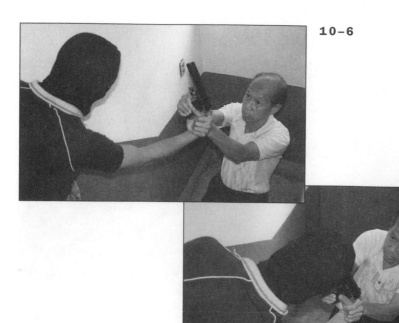

10-6

10-7

10-8

10-6 He may try to maintain his balance by leaning back; you can follow his energy by turning his wrist and applying pressure toward him.

10-7 Continue applying pressure.

10-8 Your right hand sweeps back to disarm him; be sure to take a few steps down to maintain a safe distance.

→ SERIES 11 ←

Here is another disadvantageous position that still leaves you within the correct range to counter. You may maintain this lock, or conclude with a hip throw, but remember to stay in control of the gun.

11–1 The opponent is close behind you, with his gun pointed at the right side of your head.

11–2 Push your head back to move out of the line of fire, while sliding your arm against his right arm.

11–1

11–2

11–3 Turn slightly to your right, with your left hand taking control of his gun. Be sure to wrap your thumb around the outside of the gun. Your right hand passes to the outside and applies pressure to his elbow by pushing down and using your upper arm as a fulcrum.

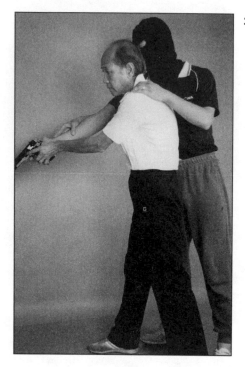

11–3

→ IV ←

TECHNIQUES WITH THE
POLICE CLUB

The police club—whether it is a *tonfa* or a simple stick—is a law enforcement officer's most basic piece of equipment, and provides the simplest form of defense. It can also be used against an armed or unarmed suspect, as it is readily available at the officer's side. Given its effectiveness and ability to control without inflicting permanent damage, police throughout the world learn police club techniques.

As in all martial arts training, the use of the police club also requires constant practice, and drilling of combat simulations. Only then will the police officer be able to use it effectively and with correct power. Given its long history, the club was originally designed to be used against a knife or another club; even so, it has many modern-day applications. As in all other combat situations, the officer must make use of good position and distance, so that when he initiates a move, he will be able to efficiently put into play what he has learned in practice. When the suspect is in a position where he cannot launch his own attack, one is fully safe and free to use appropriate means to arrest him. Of course, when faced with a suspect armed with a weapon, it is natural to be afraid. Therefore, remember that the most dangerous enemy is not the criminal, but fear itself; the best way to conquer these fears is through persistent practice with real weapons. The famous adage "old soldiers never die" could mean that those with the most experience are best equipped to handle any situation. When fear is conquered and you are fully confident in your abilities, you can calmly execute techniques.

In order to familiarize police with club techniques, the pictures depict left-to-right strikes and right-to-left strikes, which are identically delivered from either side in terms of direction and force. Easy to learn and execute, they may also be applied as blocks, strikes to a suspect's weapon hand, and leverage for use in locking, trapping, and throwing. Combining these skills with footwork, one can fully grasp the ideal of a "live" person practicing "live" martial skills and be well equipped to deal with an armed suspect.

⇾ SERIES 1 ⇽

As in unarmed combat against an armed opponent, position will often determine what techniques the suspect will use. The stick becomes an extension of the arm, giving you an extra measure of safety. Blocking with the stick is also an offensive strike, and further allows you to take control of the opponent's knife arm with your hand.

1-1 Facing in a cross-shoulder position, the knifeman stabs down-ward. Block with the stick, forming a cross with his arm.

1-2 Grasping and controlling the opponent's knife hand with your left hand, slide the stick through and around the outside of his elbow. The far end of the stick should end on your opponent's neck.

1-1

1-2

1-3   Use your opponent's forearm as a fulcrum, press down on the neck (or arm if he blocks).

1-4   Maintain control as your opponent falls to the ground.

1-3

1-4

✈ SERIES 2 ✦

The stick's simplicity allows it to be used in multiple functions, with strikes at varying angles. Notice that the block is also a strike.

2–1   Standing cross-shoulder, intercept the enemy's downward thrust with a strike to the inside of his arm.

2–2   Your left hand moves to control his knife hand, turning the wrist over in a counterclockwise motion so that his arm bends. Slide the stick over the top of his arm to behind his shoulder and under his armpit.

2–1

2–2

2-3

2-3 The far end of the stick passes through the bend in his arm and hooks on to his wrist. As you go through the motion, hold the stick and follow his turn, moving to his right.

2-4 Step back with your left leg and press down with your right hand.

2-4

➤ **SERIES 3** ⭠

The angle of deflection has changed again, but can still be used for joint locks. After the lock brings down the opponent, the stick is reversed to pin his arm down.

3-1   As your opponent stabs downward, step to your left and deflect with the stick. The inside of your fist should be facing you, while the stick faces outward and slightly down.

3-2   Use your left hand to control your opponent's knife hand at the wrist, sliding the stick around his arm and behind the elbow.

3-1

3-2

3-3 The far end of the stick should come to rest behind your left wrist to use for a lever and lock his arm; step forward to increase the pressure on his joint.

3-4 Use the butt of the stick to contact his arm (or neck if he doesn't block).

3-5 Press downward to force him down.

3-3

3-4

3-5

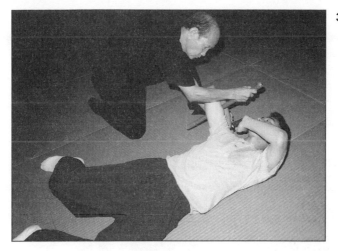

3-6

3-6 As you turn the stick over with a pulling motion to pressure his forearm down to the floor, the other end of the stick should be beneath his upper arm.

3-7 Disarm.

3-7

⇢ SERIES 4 ⇠

You do not necessarily need to end with a joint lock or throw. Here, the stick is used in combination with techniques to attack the suspect's knife hand, thereby keeping the knife at a distance.

4–1

4–2

4–1 As he slashes downward in a 45-degree cutting motion across his body, block to the inside of his knife hand with an outward sweep of your stick; the stick should be pointed slightly downward. Maintain a guard with your left hand.

4–2 Cut downward to the inside of his wrist with the blade of your left hand, while chambering the stick…

4–3 For another strike to the inside of his forearm. Twist your waist with the blow to increase power.

4–3

⊰ SERIES 5 ⊱

Combined with footwork, your stick strikes can come at different angles to varying targets.

5-1   Standing cross-shoulder, bleed off his downward knife-thrust with the butt of the stick up.

5-2   Side-step to your left while sliding the stick down his arm and striking at the front of his knee.

5-1

5-2

5-3   Getting behind him, strike with a wide sweeping motion to the back of his hand.

5-3

✦ SERIES 6 ✦

This technique resembles Knife Series 1, with the stick acting as an extension of the arm. When the stick is pressed into nerve centers, its hardness makes it all the more effective.

6-1 Facing off shoulder-to-shoulder against your opponent...

6-2 As he thrusts downward. . .

6-1

6-2

6–3   Use your left hand to block the inside of his knife wrist while using the stick to hit behind his upper arm with a backhand flick of the wrist. You should press his hand outward with your left hand, while the stick slides behind his forearm.

6–4   As the stick passes upward, grab the other end of the stick with your left hand, so as to lock your wrist with his.

6–3

6–4

6–5 Twist over in a sharp motion.

6–6 (close-up, reverse angle)

6–5

6–6

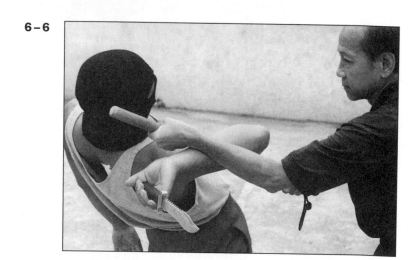

⇥ **SERIES 7** ⇤

This series once again demonstrates the versatility in striking with the stick.

7–1   Facing off shoulder-to-shoulder with your opponent...

7–2   As he hacks at you, step to the right while stabbing forward with your stick.

7–1

7–2

7–3 Strike to the knee as you step again to your right.

7–4 As he falls forward, follow up with a downward strike to the back of his head.

7–3

7–4

→ SERIES 8 ←

Strikes to the weapon hand, particularly on the inside of the wrist, may cause the opponent to lose his grip on his weapon.

8-1 Facing off as the opponent chambers to strike with a downward slash...

8-2 Pivot to your right and out of the line of his slash with a stab to his ribs.

8-1

8-2

8–3

8–3 Follow up with a hard strike to the right arm...

8–4 Forcing him to drop his knife.

8–4

⊹ SERIES 9 ⊹

Once again, the strikes of the stick are combined with footwork to create an efficient barrage of attacks.

9-1 Facing off shoulder to shoulder...

9-2 Step outside to your left while striking to the back of his wrist.

9-1

9-2

9-3 Follow up with a right step forward and a hit to the kneecap.

9-4 Stepping behind him, use a sweeping motion. . .

9-3

9-4

9-5   To hit him in the back of the neck.

9-5

⇥ V ⇤

UNARMED COMBAT

Given their line of work, law enforcement officers must sometimes face violent criminals. At such times, physical struggle is often unavoidable, and thus preparatory training in unarmed combat is imperative. Naturally, if time permits, I recommend systematic training in Wing Chun kung fu, given its great martial power and structural advantages in close-range combat. On the other hand, constraints of time or limited interest in this traditional Chinese martial art may render learning it impracticable.

Therefore for this course in peace officer combat training, I have taken the principles of Wing Chun kung fu as a basis, and chosen effective techniques that are easily linked with the body's natural movements. Furthermore, with growing concerns about the police taking extreme measures in stressful situations, Wing Chun shares the liabilities of any martial style that emphasizes deadly striking skills. Its arsenal of hits to the eyes, throat, and other vital areas, while perhaps suitable before the existence of organized law enforcement, can have legal consequences in a society governed by the rule of law. Thus, I have also adopted the joint-locking and throwing skills of Asian fighting arts for use in controlling and arresting a suspect. These techniques are easily integrated with Wing Chun's offensive and defensive structure, and follow Wing Chun's guiding principles.

Aside from developing skilled technique and familiarity with actual fighting, police personnel must also undergo a related curriculum of education, body conditioning, and martial skills. When lacking personal knowledge of the perpetrator, you must not only possess fighting skills but also an understanding of military strategy. If you can place yourself in the best strategic position to defeat the opponent, or lure the enemy into a disadvantageous fighting situation or position, you have already won half the battle. Police officers should carefully integrate movement with strategy and avoid impulsive action in the process of capturing a suspect. Otherwise, it is easy to make an inopportune movement or put oneself in a disadvantageous position.

When all is said and done, overeagerness to strike usually results in leaving yourself vulnerable to attack. You should adopt a vigorous but conservative approach based upon close observation, and matching action/reaction to the particulars of the situation. In other words, if the opponent does not move first, look for appropriate opportunities before making your own movement. If the opponent does attack immediately, then respond aggressively in an appropriate manner.

Once again, it cannot be overemphasized that when dealing with live opponents one risks everything by employing theatrical movement or relying upon speed, strength, or "dead" movement. This is for the simple reason that your opponent is a fully involved participant and not a member of some audience there for a spectacle. Fighting a capable criminal opponent is a very serious affair and not a game.

OPEN HAND TECHNIQUES

⇢ SERIES 1 ⇠

Using Wing Chun's contact reflexes, one can move quickly from striking range to throwing range.

1–1 Standing shoulder-to-shoulder, when the opponent punches with his right hand, intercept his punch with a left inside block.

1–2 Step in with your right leg to shift position, while thrusting your right hand toward the opponent's triceps. Your arm should pin his left hand.

1–1

1–2

1-3 Step back with your left leg while pressing your body into his body.

1-4 Turn your body to execute a hip throw to...

1-5 Throw your opponent down.

1-3

1-4

1-5

1-6 While your opponent is on the ground, apply pressure and control his elbow joint by pulling up with your right hand and pushing down with the left.

1-7 Continuing the motion, twist his arm backward...

1-8 Into a prone hammer lock; push your knee into his lower back for further control.

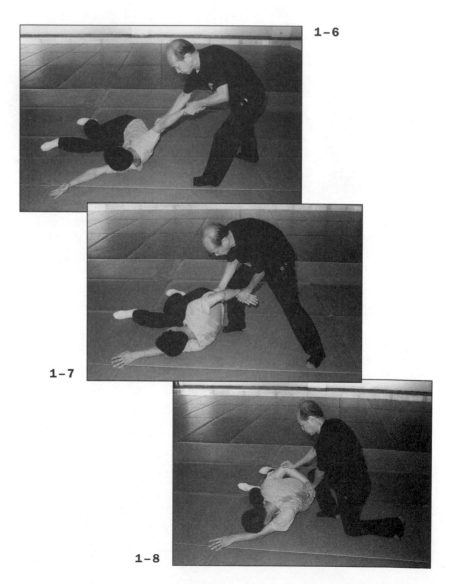

1-6

1-7

1-8

⊹ SERIES 2 ⊹

This technique is essentially Stick Series 1, without the stick. Notice how adherence to Wing Chun techniques allows you to feel where your opponent's hands are at all times.

2–1 Standing shoulder-to-shoulder, intercept and stick to the opponent's right-hand punch.

2–2 Lock the enemy's other arm by thrusting forward with a right arm-bar.

2–1

2–2

2–3 Push your left hand forward to push his right hand into him, thread your right arm behind his, and lock to your forearm; your right arm is a lever.

2–4 (close-up) Press down while starting to kneel.

2–3

2–4

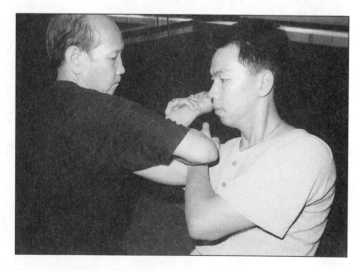

2-5 Maintaining the same position, sink forward so that you are kneeling on your right knee, forcing him down...

2-6 And causing him to lose his balance.

2-5

2-6

2-7

2-7 Slide your right arm out and use it to push and control his elbow.

2-8 As he naturally turns to his side to resist the lock, use your left hand to push his wrist into his back, while pulling his elbow toward you.

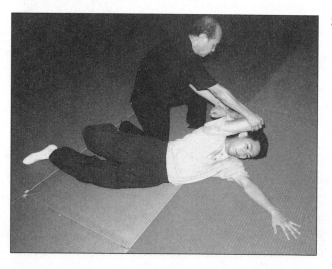

2-8

⤳ SERIES 3 ⤶

Here is a different technique, used when moving in the cross-shoulder position. Notice the flow of locks, from an elbow lock to a hammer lock.

3-1 Standing cross-shoulder and slightly to your left side, intercept his right punch with your own right outside block.

3-2 Step in with your left leg and pull and twist his arm around so his elbow is facing up.

3-1

3-2

3-3

3-3 Your left elbow wraps over the attacker's arm at the elbow joint and clamps down.

3-4 While your left hand controls his wrist, use your right hand to thread through the bend in his elbow.

3-4

3-5 Step back to his rear and maintain control at his shoulder joint with your right hand while holding firmly to his wrist with your other hand.

3-6 Kneel down for control.

3-6

✦ SERIES 4 ✦

Similar to Knife Series 11 and Gun Series 7, this technique may also be applied to unarmed combat. Your locks once again flow, starting from an elbow breaker, then stepping out into a wrist lock, and finally threading through into a shoulder lock.

4-1 Against a right punch...

4-2 Step to the left so that you are standing shoulder-to-shoulder, and block to the outside with your right arm.

4-1

4-2

4–3   Slide under the opponent's outstretched arm with your left hand while stepping in with the left leg.

4–4   Turn your body toward the opponent while your left arm returns to the opponent's wrist, then pull down, using your left shoulder as a fulcrum.

4–5   Step back out with your left leg, while turning your own arms left over right.

4–3

4–4

4–5

4–6   Fnished position.

4–7   Your left hand threads on the inside the opponent's arm, wrapping upward so that your hand is on his shoulder joint.

4–8   Step back with your right leg and lock the shoulder joint; his wrist should be locked in the crook of your elbow.

4–6

4–7

4–8

ALTERNATELY, FROM STEP 4-3

Instead of using your hand to thread through your opponent's arm, you can use your knee to apply pressure to the joint.

4-4b Turn your body toward the opponent while your left arm returns to his wrist; pull down, using your left shoulder as a fulcrum.

4-5b Pivot out with your left leg, twist his wrist over (see 4-5 above), keeping his arm straight, then push his arm into his body.

4-6b Push your knee into his elbow joint.

4-4b

4-5b

4-6b

✦ SERIES 5 ✦

Demonstration of a simple wrapping hands technique from Wing Chun's first form, executed from a wrist lock:

5-1   Stepping to the left so that you are cross-shoulder, deflect his forward right punch with your right hand.

5-2   Take control of his wrist with both of your hands and twist his fist over clockwise.

5-1

5-2

5–3 Step in with your left foot while your right hand threads inside of his elbow joint.

5–4 Step forward with your right foot as you lock your right arm into his shoulder joint.

5–3

5–4

5–5 Kneel forward while maintaining your upper body position.

5–5

⇥ VI ⇤

TECHNIQUES
AGAINST A BAT

⇥ SERIES 1 ⇤

Although different in function and use, the bat's line of attack is similar to that of a long blade. However, its bluntness allows for it to be used against the opponent after you have redirected its initial energy. Notice the use of the Wing Chun kuan sao, a technique effective at stopping high round-house kicks. In the end, you are using the bat against its wielder.

1-1

1-1   Facing shoulder-to-shoulder, step forward with your left leg as the opponent chambers his bat.

1-2 Jam his bat using a Wing Chun kuan sao (left hand up to protect the face, with right arm bent roughly parallel to the ground; your arms should be in contact to reinforce the structure of your position), turning slightly to the left to bleed off the force of the bat.

1-3 Your right hand pushes the bat back over his left shoulder.

1-2

1-3

1-4 Step in with your left foot to finish pressing the bat into his neck.

1-5 Your left hand thrusts behind the other side of his hand. . .

1-4

1-5

1-6 To take hold of the other side of the bat. His head should be between your arms.

1-6

ALTERNATELY, FROM STEP 1-5

Instead of grabbing the bat, you may use the crook of your elbow to hold it down, while using your hand to press your opponent's head into a choke hold.

1–6b Wrap your left arm around the top of the bat...

1–7b And push on the right side of your opponent's head.

1–6b

1–7b

1–8b Apply pressure down on his head.

1–9b (close-up)

1–8b

1–9b

✦ **SERIES 2** ✦

Using the Wing Chun principle of simultaneous attack and defense, you combine the kuan sao with a kick to the knee.

2-1 Step forward with your left leg as your opponent chambers his bat.

2-2 Jam his bat using a Wing Chun kuan sao, turning slightly to the left to bleed off the bat.

2-1

2-2

2–3 Deliver a right kick to his right knee.

2–4 As you step down, drop your right elbow to pull the bat down, and stretch forward with your left hand to grab the back of his neck.

2–3

2–4

2-5   Push his neck down while swiping the bat away.

2-5

ABOUT THE TRANSLATORS

Bradley Temple studied Wing Chun kung fu under Lo Man Kam in Taiwan, the Republic of China. After living in Taiwan for ten years, he and his Chinese wife, Alexandra, currently reside in Las Vegas, Nevada, where he teaches Wing Chun. Temple has a certificate in acupuncture and is an accomplished Chen Taiji enthusiast, having studied in Zhenzhou, China, under a 19th generation master of the Chen family, Chen Pei-ju. He has won awards in martial arts competitions in Asia and the United States.

Nicholas Veitch was introduced to Wing Chun by Francis Szeto before undertaking serious study in Taiwan under Lo Man Kam from 1995 to 1998. Nick lived in Taiwan for nine years, working in a miscellany of professions before settling upon translation and essay writing.

John Kang started martial arts training at age ten, having learned Wu and Chen style Taiji and Shaolin martial arts before moving in 1995 to Taiwan and studying Wing Chun kung fu under Lo Man Kam. He has worked as a translator in the Taipei branch of a prominent Japanese securities company.

http://wingchun.iscool.net